GW01161823

QUATRAINS

Echoes of Existence

❖

ILLUSTRATED IN THE STYLE OF EDMUND DULAC

C.S. DOUGLAS

EVERLY BOOKS
PUBLISHING CO.

New York   Boston   London   Paris   Toronto

EVERLY BOOKS
PUBLISHING CO.
Copyright © 2007 – 2023 by Chris Sebastian Douglas

All rights reserved by the author. Except where permitted under the United States Copyright Act of 1976, no part of this publication may be reproduced or distributed in any form or by any means or stored on a database or retrieval system without prior written permission from the publisher.

PUBLISHED IN CANADA

ISBN 978-1-7772781-6-8

PUBLISHER'S NOTE

This is a book of verses. Without limiting the rights under copyright reserved above, no part of this publication may be reproduced, stored in, or introduced into a retrieval system or transmitted in any form or by any means (electronic, mechanical, photocopying, recording, or otherwise) without the prior written permission of both the copyright owner and the above publisher of this book.

The scanning, uploading, and distributing of this book via the Internet or any other means without the publisher's permission is illegal and legally punishable. Please purchase only authorized electronic editions and do not participate in or encourage electronic piracy or copyrighted materials. Your support of the author's rights is very much appreciated.

Color illustrations in the style of Edmund Dulac Designs by C.S. Douglas made in MidJourney.

Cover design by Chris S. Douglas/Everly Books Publishing Co.

To Nicole and Ioana

ACKNOWLEDGMENTS

I thank my father, John Sebastian Douglas, for opening the wisdom box for me at the age of seven when he recited verses from the Rubaiyat of Omar Khayyam and later for encouraging me to publish the quatrains I wrote and kept secret as my personal diary for almost four decades. I would have probably never published them had I not inadvertently found the last letter he wrote to me before his death, in which he reminds me not to forget to keep writing and publishing these verses. And if this isn't fate, look at how I am paying homage to him right now as I fulfill his wishes today, October 4th, the day he of his trip into another dimension.

Many thanks go to my English friend, poet, and novelist, Dawn G. Torrens, who promised me, in her noble and delicate way of putting it, that if I would publish this book, she would add her sincere critique review for the back of the cover. How could I refuse such an offer? Dawn is the author of *Amelia's Story* trilogy, a gem of a tale, as of many other books, most of them novels, the latest entitled *One for Sorrow*. I asked Dawn with timidity if she thought our poet friend and Radio host, painter, composer, and novelist, Lee Benson, could give me a review should I dare send him my podcast intro episode. And thanks to Dawn, I reached Lee, to whom otherwise I would have never sent my verses as I know him a pretentious literary critic, and therefore didn't want to spoil his reputation.

I left Lee Benson last because I would like to thank him for suggesting I print what he heard in sound. Lee, known for books such as *No Naked Walls* and *The True Tale of Rotton Towers*, also helped me choose from Edmund Dulac's style color illustrations I had produced with MidJourney during the few sleepless nights I am used to having lately. (Thank you, MidJourney, for reading my mind and printing the color masterpieces).

I thank the Universe for contributing to my fate and my eternal old friend Omar Khayyam for visiting me and inspiring my thoughts when I write. I say old friend... since I am now at his age.

Preface

"*Quatrains: Echoes of Existence*" emerges as a resplendent constellation of quatrains meticulously composed by the renowned American poet and writer of Romanian-German descent, C.S. Douglas, full name Chris Sebastian Douglas. Drawing substantive inspiration from the ethereal brilliance of Omar Khayyam's celebrated Rubaiyat, Douglas elegantly weaves verses reflective of the Omaric meter, cleverly injecting his own stylistic nuances and rhythmic distinctiveness to disrupt any latent monotony, sometimes opting for a divergent rhyming structure. Although reminiscent of Khayyam's works, this stylistic amalgamation births a composition that distinctly establishes its unique aesthetic and intellectual identity.

Every quatrain in this illustrious collection is a reflective prism, capturing the diverse hues of life's moments and experiences, encapsulating Douglas's philosophical musings and poignant reflections spanning four decades. This journey began as whispers of the soul, intimate expressions never meant to transcend the privacy of their creation, shared only amidst scholarly discourses and philosophical debates with close friends, often presented anonymously.

Much like Edward FitzGerald, who initially published merely two hundred copies of his translation of Omar Khayyam's Rubaiyat and placed them in the Piccadilly antiquarian fourpence box where it was discovered by

Dante Gabriel Rossetti, Douglas's journey with his quatrains underwent a transformative odyssey. The discovery of a persuasive letter from his father, John Sebastian — whose name Sebastian proudly incorporates as his middle name after his father died in 1999 — became the catalyst for bringing these quatrains to the world. The letter, filled with paternal wisdom, suggested that the quatrains resonated with the essence of Khayyam's Rubaiyat, a timeless fountain of inspiration for global poets, urging their publication.

Embarking on a meticulous expedition through over four hundred of his verses, Douglas distilled them to two hundred exemplary quatrains. He extended their essence into the realms of audiobooks and podcasts, enriched with the resonant timbre of a professional actor, and visually complemented with illustrations reminiscent of Edmund Dulac's captivating style, mirroring the aesthetic symmetry of FitzGerald's edition. This masterful convergence of lyrical, auditory, and visual artistry offers readers an immersive, multi-sensory exploration of poetic expression.

To exemplify, ponder upon the following quatrain:

> *"With every day that passes by*
> *A young man's born, an old man dies.*
> *And thousand stars await its turn*
> *To go, and never to return."*

In this lyrical gem, Douglas demonstrates his prowess in succinctly portraying the ephemeral and cyclical essence of life and the cosmos, a cornerstone of Omaric poetics.

However, he injects his ethos, exploring the inevitable dance of life and death and the looming shadow of oblivion, subtly whispering to readers the timeless wisdom of embracing the present.

This splendid collection, therefore, stands not merely as a homage to the timeless elegance of Omar Khayyam's Rubaiyat but as a beacon of modern poetic and philosophical reflection, narrating the myriad 'echoes of existence' through the refined lens of C.S. Douglas's profound insights and distinctive articulation.

In its pages, readers will find a harmonious symphony of thoughts and emotions, an exploration of the intricate tapestry of life, inviting contemplation, resonance, and introspective discovery. It is a literary odyssey, a ballet of words and wisdom, a mosaic of existential echoes resounding through the corridors of thought and time.

Douglas's quatrains transcend the aesthetic allure of rhythmic verses, evolving into philosophical reverberations echoing the myriad facets of reality, life, and the human experience. Each quatrain could be perceived as an isolated chapter in a memoir, exploring varied spectrums of life and emotion, inviting the reader into a dance of introspection and revelation, and dwelling in the metaphysical spaces where divine proof is sought within the self rather than in the external realms of superstition and speculation.

In this journey, Douglas encourages a life that harmonizes Epicurean pursuit of pleasure with a moral and ethical compass, steering clear of hedonistic excesses and maintaining a sophisticated balance rooted in honor and integrity. He weaves subtle philosophical tapestries within his verses, drawing the reader into reflective contemplation.

Consider, for example, the quatrain:

> *"Time flies like an arrow in the sky;*
> *We watch it pass and wonder where it flies,*
> *Waste not a second but rush and grab the gift*
> *To live, and love, and laugh, then say goodbye."*

Here, Douglas illustrates the transient and elusive nature of time, urging a passionate embrace of the present, a relishing of life's pleasures, and an unreserved experience of emotions before the inevitable farewell that time dictates, reminiscent of the carpe diem theme found in many classical works.

In another verse:

> *"Your body next to mine in an eternal hold,*
> *A glass of wine of red grape to uphold*
> *From dusk till dawn, our Hearts and Selves will blend*
> *To write the best love story ever told."*

The poet explores the intimate intertwinement of beings, the blending of souls in a narrative of passion and unity, penned with the ink of shared experiences and mutual discoveries under the watchful eyes of the stars. It is a delicate portrayal of love, resonating with the subtleties of shared being, transcending mere physicality to enter the realm of the eternal.

Moreover, Douglas addresses themes of humanity and morality, as illustrated in the quatrain:

> *"And so, you lashed your fellow man with bane,*
> *And left him in a trail of blood and pain,*
> *— Have you just, for a moment, contemplate*
> *The Price you'll pay for all your Selfish Gain?"*

This quatrain vividly portrays the consequences of malice and self-centered pursuits, inviting contemplation on the moral cost and the repercussions of such actions. It is a stark reminder of the inherent ethical responsibility within human interactions and the moral debts accrued through acts of cruelty and greed.

Beyond the ethical and moral, his quatrains plunge into the mysteries of the essence, the cosmos, and the metaphysical realms, intertwining philosophical musings with observations of the natural world and the mysteries of the universe.

For example:

> _*"The stars are shining in the vault of Heaven*
> *The moon is smiling on the earth below*
> *'Tell, what are these to me who seek the truth*
> *What lies beyond the realm of sight and show?"*_

This quatrain captures a quest for understanding, a pursuit of truths beyond the tangible and visible world, probing into the essence of nature and the unknown realms beyond the seen universe. It reflects mankind's eternal quest for knowledge and understanding, a journey into the labyrinth of the Soul to uncover the truths hidden within its intricate walls.

In another, he reflects on the transient nature of life and beauty, represented by the blooming rose and the singing nightingale, touching upon themes of mortality and the fleeting nature of being, as seen in the quatrain:

> *"And so the Rose that's blooming in its fair*
> *Inspires the nightingale concerting his mate;*
> *Lo! How the Rose will fade and disappear*
> *And how his Soul, like mine, shall mourn his Fate."*

This presents a poignant reminder of the ephemeral beauty of life and the inevitable progression of time, underscoring the impermanent nature of our reality and the constant interplay of life and death, creation and decay.

Douglas also addresses the human spirit and the internal battles we all face, emphasizing the value of perseverance and courage, as reflected in:

> *"You may have Failed a Thousand Fails before*
> *Wanting to give it up, shutting the door;*
> *Oh, let not have your Fears define your Fate*
> *For once a Winner, you'll be poor—no more."*

This quatrain imparts wisdom on the resilience of the human spirit and the transformative power of overcoming one's fears, reflecting a philosophical depth and an understanding of the human condition akin to the timeless wisdom found in ancient philosophical texts.

The quatrain:

> "Upon this endless stage where Fate and Daydreams chase
> In this Life's fleeting twirls as round and round we pace
> Let this be our anthem to share with the youth
> "Be ashamed to die without a Victory for Human Race."

Here, Douglas sends a powerful message of legacy, responsibility, and the pursuit of a life of significance, challenging the reader to leave a positive impact on the world and to strive for victories that elevate humanity.

Like Edward Fitzgerald or Richard Le Gallienne before him, C.S. Douglas is not merely a transcriber of philosophical musings but a weaver of thought, a craftsman molding the clay of lifeblood into intricate shapes of understanding and reflection. In "Quatrains: Echoes of Existence," he invites readers to embark on a journey through the kaleidoscope of life, to contemplate the multifaceted reflections of actuality, and to savor the rich fabric of experiences that define the human condition. The quatrains are not mere verses but are echoes of the vast symphony of life, each one resonating with its unique melody, inviting readers to listen, reflect, and understand the harmonies and dissonances of life.

> "In this Great Expanse of endless Stars and Gleam
> The Universe itself: an endless Stretching Dream
> Of timeless boundaries. And yet, my friend—

> *Behold!*
> *There's something even larger—Stupidity*
> *Extreme..."*

With such verses, Douglas portrays the boundless enormity of the universe and contrasts it humorously with the seemingly limitless bounds of human folly, prompting readers to reflect on the juxtaposition of the grandiosity of the cosmos and the often trivial and absurd pursuits of mankind.

> *"For such is LIFE—a canvas sprinkled with*
> *Hopes and Treasures*
> *Alike a Turkish carpet — a Caravan of Pleasures*
> *Where you and I get oft 'n lost yet find ourselves again*
> *In Eve's and Adam's clothes —poor Angels without feathers."*

Here, life is depicted as a colorful canvas of experiences, a journey through pleasures and discoveries where we continually find and lose ourselves, a playful reference to the human experience, reminiscent of the biblical Adam and Eve, with their innocence and naked truths.

This particular following verse is an intricate amalgamation of homage, conversation, revelation, and muse-like inspiration, eloquently intertwining the ethereal presence of Omar Khayyam with the poetics of the writer.

> *"Khayyam! You fooled me my old friend*
> *When said you'll go and 'that's the end';*
> *Last night while writing, as a sign*

You helped my verse and poured me wine."

The initial line, *"Khayyam! You fooled me my old friend,"* immediately reveals a sense of camaraderie, a poetic alliance across time and space with the celebrated Persian poet, mathematician, and astronomer Omar Khayyam. It portrays an intimate, conversational tone, depicting a friendly reproach, implying a sense of playful deception.

"When said you'll go and 'that's the end';" is a contemplation on the transient nature of life and the seeming finality of being as perceived by Khayyam. This line accentuates the initial playful reproach and underscores the paradox of mortality and perpetual presence, hinting at a transcendental continuation beyond the corporal confines of life, a metaphysical quiddity where the essence of Khayyam perpetuates.

In *"Last Night while writing, as a sign,"* the poet suggests a transcendental moment of connection, a metaphysical interaction between the poet and Khayyam. It reflects an ephemeral, nocturnal inspiration, a sign from beyond, emphasizing the silent, mystical communication between the sage of the past and the poet of the present.

"You helped my verse and poured me wine." This concluding line beautifully amalgamates the ethereal assistance with the corporeal joy of wine, symbolizing both inspiration and celebration. Here, wine is not just a literal indulgence but a metaphorical infusion of poetic elation and divine creativity. It depicts a scenario where the celestial and the earthly intertwine, where Khayyam's essence aids in the birth of poetry while bestowing the

earthly pleasure of wine.

This verse is not merely a melodic arrangement of words but a refined, intellectual liaison between two poets separated by the sands of time yet united in thought and expression. It is a sophisticated dialogue that traverses the tangible and the intangible, merging Khayyam's philosophical wisdom with the modern writer's poetic pen. It serves as a splendid reminder of the timeless and boundless nature of poetic thoughts, transcending temporal limitations and physical barriers, allowing a seamless flow of ideas and inspirations across the epochs. It's a rich, nuanced exploration of poetic lineage and metaphysical connectivity, creating an elegant symphony of words that resonate with eternal echoes of existence and artistic symbiosis.

I will end with this quatrain notably rich in metaphysical and moral exploration, contemplating the inherent dichotomy of Right and Wrong and the existential consequences of such choices:

> *"Whatever you may choose: The Right or Wrong*
> *Your Book of Life, when finished, shall belong*
> *To the Eternal Library, entire chapters all.*
> *In favor of the Master of Your Soul."*

The first line immediately establishes a tone of universal applicability, proposing a moral dilemma intrinsic to human nature, highlighting the eternal battle between virtue and vice that every individual must navigate through.

The quatrain represents life as a "Book," a metaphor suggesting that our lives are a compilation of narratives filled with choices and consequences, each chapter a testament to our moral and ethical journeys. The mention of the "Eternal Library" implies a collective reservoir of human experiences and moralities, possibly suggesting a transcendental or metaphysical realm where the sagas of human souls are archived.

The last line concludes with a powerful contemplation on accountability and spiritual autonomy, "In favor of the Master of Your Soul." This phrase suggests an ultimate spiritual reckoning, possibly implicating the self as the master, where the individual is accountable for the choices made. It could also imply a higher entity or a divine figure as the "Master," indicating a final judgment or valuation of one's life based on one's moral and ethical actions.

Moreover, the choice between "The Right or Wrong" and the resultant submission of one's "Book of Life" to the "Eternal Library" reflects the intricate interplay between free will and destiny, moral choice, and cosmic consequence, offering readers a profound insight into the philosophical and existential dimensions of morality and the human journey. The quatrain, thus, invites readers to reflect on the moral and philosophical dimensions of their actions and the legacy they contribute to the eternal, metaphysical weaving of esse.

This quatrain's elegance and depth mark it as a sophisticated blend of philosophical inquiry and poetic expression, a testament to the author's capacity to encapsulate complex existential questions within a quatrain's concise and eloquent form.

The collection is a mélange of reflections, observations, wisdom, humor, and poignant truths, drawing readers into a dance of words and thoughts, of echoes and silences, painting the myriad shades of sentience with the brushstrokes of his pen. The work is a testament to Douglas's profound insight into the human spirit, the world, and the mysteries of the universe, offering readers a mirror to reflect upon their own lives, thoughts, and experiences.

In "Quatrains: Echoes of Existence," Douglas offers a wealth of philosophical and poetic richness, presenting an exquisite blend of visual, auditory, and intellectual artistry, weaving a tapestry of thought that is as enlightening as it is enchanting. Douglas opens a window to a world where every line is a journey, every word a universe, inviting us to look, see, think, and feel, explore the depths of our being, and echo the timeless reflections of life.

In conclusion, "Quatrains: Echoes of Existence" is more than a collection of verses; it is a poetic odyssey through the realms of thought, emotion, and survival, a beacon of light in the vast expanse of the human experience, inviting readers to navigate the intricate pathways of life and to echo the whispers of existence in their hearts.

—Adam Incognito

Forward

A literary polymath and a connoisseur of the arts, C.S. Douglas navigates through the expansive domains of writing, poetry, and entrepreneurial ventures with effortless eloquence. With roots tracing back to Romanian, Czech, German, and Scottish origins, Douglas imbues his works with a rich tapestry of cultural and philosophical musings.

As the founder of AUTHORPAEDIA® — "The World's Only Encyclopedia Dedicated to Authors," and the dynamic force behind AuthorTV®, he has sculpted platforms that celebrate and scrutinize the literary world. His entrepreneurial spirit and humanitarian endeavors reflect a deep-seated commitment to both the tangible and abstract facets of continuation and creativity.

Douglas, not just a poet but a novelist, translator, screenwriter, and playwright, demonstrates a deft hand across varied literary forms, synthesizing them into his own style. His quatrains in "Quatrains: Echoes of Existence," while nodding to the philosophical depth reminiscent of Omar Khayyam, carry their own unique timbre and thematic explorations, traversing the metaphysical, the tangible, and the enigmatically existential.

A musical lyricist, composer, and once the host of the AUTHORPADIA LIVE Show at AuthorTV, Douglas continues to weave his varied experiences into his writings, crafting narratives and verses that explore, celebrate, and question the myriad facets of life and beyond.

J.S.D.

QUATRAINS—ECHOES OF EXISTENCE

QUATRAINS

Echoes of Existence

QUATRAINS—ECHOES OF EXISTENCE

I

With every day that passes by

A young man's born, an old man dies.

And thousand stars await its turn

To go and never to return.

II

Enjoy the minute of *Today*

Tomorrow it may be too late,

For *Life* and *Death* are old time friends

And *endless games* they like to play.

III

To Sing, and Play, and Love, and Breathe,

To Sleep, and Eat, and to Enjoy

The Life that's given – Not a toy

To be amused of – *Careful please!*

IV

A woman of your dreams in a *Garden of Eden*,

A *Tree of Knowledge* and a *Fruit Forbidden*;

Beware though—The thirst of *Wisdom* at the sight of Love

Had nailed the *Ten Commandments* way down and *Above*.

V

For here I come to see the *World*

Rotate its ways and life unfold;

And *one-way* only does it move

And I with it, so I was told.

VI

Do not forget my dear friend,

From *Earth* you came and shall descend

Why bother measuring the time?

There's *No Beginning* and *No End*.

VII

And when you'll realize you're *Old* and *Grey*

Rewind your thoughts to that regretting day,

And call my name, and I shall be descending

To whisper in your ear – I love you to a never-ending!

VIII

Don't question "*Why*," but try to be
Yourself with many lonely dreams
Where memories come back and stay
And ' thousand years a minute seems.

IX

Your walks and figure shall attract attention
For all desire your body to enjoy,
To *Love*, and *Kiss*, and *Play* and *Pull* and *Reap*
And then to leave your heart an empty deep.

X

Twist and twine the *Life is winding*

As we seem so far away

And yet so close to the *final answer*

Which divides the *night* and *day*.

XI

As I retreated in' the fields

I heard a *thunder-voice*, and confused

I looked to where the calling came:

Don't play with fire; you shall lose!

XII

To love in dreams and then to keep

The *ever-loved* forever near,

You shall awake and search in fear

A hopeless search of timeless deep.

XIII

Young, much too young, I had to be to fall

For that pretended *Infinite* on which we roll;

Disgusted now, I watch my flying years

Betray my love for life and steal it all.

XIV

Forget the *Stress*, the *Problems*, and the *Grief*
And let our body floating like a leaf,
The wind shall sway you to your destined lane:
Ignore the Stain, the Problems, and the Pain!

XV

Look in the mirror and watch the *time*
Running backwards – *What a scold!*
For in your image, you might feel
You're getting young when getting old...

XVI

As I embraced this woman with desire

Her ways had conquered of my soul entire,

And in those moments, happily, have I thrown

A world of great importance into fire.

XVII

From way beyond and far away
They see a world rotate its rotten
And to their callow they convey
What constellation had forgotten.

XVIII

You're Born. Observe. You play. You Grow.
You Learn, You Touch. You Feel. You Know.
You Like. You Think. You Taste. You Try.
You Love. You worry. Create. And Die.

XIX

Confused? And so am I, *Confused*!
But never lost my *Love* and *Hope*;
When Life is getting rough and slope,
About my *End*, I am amused.

XX

The chestnut trees and lilacs in bloom

Near your window open to shadow your room.

A woman to love, a bosom to roll:

A *perfect combination* of *Body* and *Soul.*

XXI

Generations! Generations
Young at heart – Where did they run?
Future Hopes and *Revelations*
Thoughtful minds—*Where have you gone?*

XXII

Before reincarnation, the soul had simply asked

For one more whimsy second into the Universe to last;

And from the whole Eternity where zillions of planets lie

He looked upon the puzzling earth and into flesh was born to die.

QUATRAINS—ECHOES OF EXISTENCE

QUATRAIN 1 p. 1
[First Color Illustrated Edition]

With every day that passes by
A young man's born, an old man dies.
And thousand stars await its turn
To go and never to return.

QUATRAINS—ECHOES OF EXISTENCE

QUATRAIN IV p. 4
[First Color Illustrated Edition]

A woman of your dreams in a *Garden of Eden*,
A *Tree of Knowledge* and a *Fruit Forbidden*;
Beware, though—The thirst of *Wisdom* at the sight of Love
Had nailed the *Ten Commandments* way down and *Above*.

XXIII

What is God? I'll be a fool to say for certain

No one ever came from where they went behind that curtain;

But I can tell you this, my friend: "Don't look too far for Him

Creation is within Your Self. The Master is Within!"

XXIV

Don't Lie. Don't Scoff. Don't Hate. Don't Kill.

Don't Rape. Don't Hit someone. Don't Envy, and Don't Steal.

Don't boast. Don't look for Fame. Your passions do not treasure;

Don't sell your Soul, your heart, your body, for a passing pleasure.

XXV

Help them anytime you can,

Smile at *Destiny* now and then,

Build up *Goals* and *Sweet Beliefs*

And then, *let go*—Like Autumn's leaves.

XXVI

You need a friend, but who's to say
Whom by your side a lifetime be
When you betrayed by *Destiny*
Will kneel down, and weep, and pray?

XXVII

You're nothing but a *Motion Image*
A *Film* that's rolled a different way,
A *story* ending like all stories
Wherein new *actors* come and play.

XXVIII

It seems that far beyond and long ago

We left our youth in an immortal show;

The *thread* which splits *reality* from *real dreams*

Makes way for *you to come* and *I to go*...

XXIX

You'll add *my name* to your forgotten list

As if we've never met and I do not exist;

The dreams we've dreamed together—water thinned,

Shall blow from our memories just like wind...

XXX

Afraid of Life you followed up your mother

And into this *Dimension* you arrived in pain;

In doubt of an afterworld existence? Why, don't bother!

Whenever she will go, you'll follow her again.

XXXI

Life, is but an eyelash tremble
Whereby you and I have met;
You the pen and I the poet,
Wrote a page and left so humble.

XXXII

Out, page by page, upcoming days you turn.

Your *Life-Book* getting thin between the covers;

From what you learned, you'll teach unto another

And then depart. And then depart... forlorn.

QUATRAINS—ECHOES OF EXISTENCE

QUATRAIN XV p. 15
[First Color Illustrated Edition]

Look in the mirror and watch the *time*
Running backwards – *What a scold!*
For in your image you might feel
You're getting young, when getting old...

QUATRAIN XXIX p. 31
[First Color Illustrated Edition]

You'll add *my name* to your forgotten list
As if we've never met and I do not exist;
The dreams we've dreamed together—water thinned,
Shall blow from our memories just like wind...

XXXIII

Imagine *You*, into this Universe, created;
Born in a world with millions of your kind,
So lonely and of tears desiccated
Wanting a matching soul, you never seem to find.

XXXIV

Think, before you're shaking hands!
And guard yourself unto defense;
Cover your heart in silence thought
And wear the shield of sweet pretense.

XXXV

Before my mother lovely girls have sat

To pledge their love for I, but I have not

Fulfill their dreams nor quench my thirst for love.

Oh, adolescent mind—*How you forgot...*

XXXVI

Revolves the World so many a times

Regardless of its surface toil;

And man was born to *Build* and *Spoil*

Where *'God' Himself* in landscape *Signs*.

XXXVII

Self-Destruction—Genocide.

Wars and violence—*Human pride;*

The world's creation still burns within

An *Eternal Future* by fools *Denied.*

XXXVIII

And so, up to the end, the very end

You'll shuffle thoughts and still not understand

How our *Days* and *Nights* have learned to share the shy

And yet, be different every day than you and I.

XXXIX

See the blind? The blind can see

Where you'll never reach to be;

You shall never go that deep

While awake or while asleep.

XL

When someone said that friendship weighs more than gold

A fool when heard it, immediately has sold

The only friend he had, and tried to buy again

Another friend, but when announced it no one showed.

XLI

Khayyam! You fooled me my old friend
When said you'll go and *'that's the end'*;
Last night while writing, as a sign
You helped my verse and poured me wine.

XLII

One, humbly asked a *Priest* about and where to mark

The line that splits forever the *Daylight* from the *Dark;*

"*Within your chamber your soul illuminate,*

Before the night is falling, before it is too late."

QUATRAINS—ECHOES OF EXISTENCE

QUATRAIN XXXVII p. 41
[First Color Illustrated Edition]

Self-Destruction—Genocide.
Wars and violence—*Human pride*;
The world's creation still burns within
An *Eternal Future* by fools *Denied*.

QUATRAINS—ECHOES OF EXISTENCE

QUATRAIN XLI p. 45
[First Color Illustrated Edition]

Khayyam! You fooled me my old friend
When said you'll go and *'that's the end'*;
 Last night while writing, as a sign
You helped my verse and poured me wine.

XLIII

Should you be lost within your very senses

When *Charming Eyes* encourage your embraces?

Beware, though, *their* glare could be vicious

For it could break your heart in thousand pieces.

XLIV

For *Medicine*, to oust the stress
You'll make a *Cake of Life* and *dine*,
And burn a candle for each mess
You feel you're in. Then share some wine.

XLV

The *Optimist* and *Pessimist* argued again
Whether the glass was full or empty half-way in;
And so, they asked another to pick a side
And have been told: *The owner of this cup shall win!*

XLVI

Glides the moon upon the waters
And the night is falling deep;
Rest yourself and leave the problems
Far behind and sound asleep.

XLVII

Whatever you may choose: The *Right* or *Wrong*
Your *Book of Life* when finished, shall belong
To the *Eternal Library*, entire chapters all.
In favor of the *Master of Your Soul*.

XLVIII

Outside the house is snowing so heavenly and slow,
And by the fireplace our moods we gently lay
And let the heat of love into our hearts to blow,
And then, *Ten Thousand Years*, passed... *Today*.

XLIX

Your *Flesh* and *Body* anon shall disappear.
Do not be marked with wondering of fear;
Through love and hope you'll find your paradise
Halfway between the path of '*There*' and '*here.*'

L

The *Prophets* and the *Saints* have told

Unto the Youngsters and the Old

About how '*Future*' would one day become

The *highest commodity* ever sold.

LI

You see, a lifetime you must Play and Act

The *fashion* that is laid out and about,

For there's a *drama,* or some *parody* there is,

To dress your *symbol* in an *absurd tease.*

LII

The one you love, shall play in self-defense,

A *lover's game* of *sweet impertinence*,

And like your shadow, back and forth shall run,

From you and after you, the more you churn.

QUATRAINS—ECHOES OF EXISTENCE

QUATRAIN XLVII p. 53
[First Color Illustrated Edition]

Whatever you may choose: The *Right* or *Wrong*
Your *Book of Life*, when finished, shall belong
To the *Eternal Library*, entire chapters all.
In favor of the *Master of Your Soul*.

QUATRAINS—ECHOES OF EXISTENCE

QUATRAIN LVII p. 65
[First Color Illustrated Edition]

One starry evening as I sat on my porch chair
I thought I heard a mockingbird singing a prayer
Astonished as I was *he* said: "*My dear,
I only sing for those who want to hear!*"

LIII

After *rain* and *thunder*, we shall expect the *Sun*,

To wrap in warming wonders the grieving of the woods,

And then and unknown painter shall frame the doleful moods,

In an immortal masterpiece, *noticed after he's gone.*

LIV

Remorsefully, the *one* that you had chiefly trusted

Will crush your confidence and place it amongst rusted;

Shall lay your friendship on a *Scale of Time*

And sell you briefly and with comfort—for a *dime*.

LV

The people ruled by *One Man* a few

Shall be the witness of a war, anew'

The peaceful splendor of the lands will turn to horror,

While you will fight for '*What*' and die for '*Who?*'

LVI

A *Hope* they say is more than morning light

That scares the *Darkness* out of sable night

And turns the idol sands to one's desires

Where *'future dreams'* shall *conquer*, and *the Past–*
retires.

LVII

One starry evening as I sat on my porch chair,

I thought I heard a mockingbird singing a prayer.

Astonished as I was, *he* said: "My *dear,*

I only sing for those who want to hear!"

LVIII

When *Fate*, so graciously dormant shall arrive to *Choice*

Calling your name in soundless, muffled voice,

You shall depart so barren and without possessions

To meet a *Timeless Future* and *Past Generations*.

LIX

Somewhere, that Special One is waiting there for you
While drowsy thoughts may drive your Hopes way through;
Don't search for her in vain, but simply stare
For you might pass by her *while she is there*.

LX

"Who had equipped your body so full and sans defects

To tempt the very senses, while passionate love erects

For stormy 'n' yet so gentle caresses and desire

That changed the *Trail of History* and *Sinned* a world, entire?

LXI

Leave the haunting misery and the gloomy stress!
For the *Time of Torment* will arrive no less
Than the twilight glare of the destined night
Booked in *Eternity* by the *Emperor of Light*.

LXII

The *Infinite* as laid by *Nature*, should I guess

Is not more than wild, scattered, fireballs of stress,

Where the *Energies of Silence* fight for ever vacant space,

To win *more infinite*, and *You—Oh! Predestined human race...*

QUATRAINS—ECHOES OF EXISTENCE

QUATRAIN LXVIII p. 78
[First Color Illustrated Edition]

"To the *Young and Beautiful*, I propose a toast!
Now, this very moment, while the time's not lost;
Drink the *cup of pleasures* and the *cup of joys*
For the *Anguish Urn*, the *Old Age* employs."

QUATRAINS—ECHOES OF EXISTENCE

QUATRAIN LXIX p. 79
[First Color Illustrated Edition]

The *Climate of the World* will go awry,
The *Evil Sword* shall rule by *evil eye*;
And you—You *fools* who sold the *Planet's Fate*,
Shall beg *Salvation* from the *Seventh Gate*.

LXIII

What is *Life* without a charming chance

Of a new adventure or romance?

Oh! *Threats of Failure* and *Hopes of Victory*, you incite

Your shy admirers for a *Passion Night*.

LXIV

Lo and Behold! The one who hears well

Shall hear the *Tongue of Heaven* and the *Threats of Hell,*

Delimiting the *high sounds* from the *low,*

Adopting to its *Music* and its *Show.*

LXV

Life is for living, for only once you live *here*—they say;

So, make the very best of every second, *every day*.

Breathe deeply and imagine you are breathing *Life*.

Get high with *it* my friend—*Do not push it away...*

LXVI

Some lovers their *Names* and *Hearts*, inscribe

Upon a young tree trunk "*Forever to Survive.*"

Their marks long after they '*depart*' shall grow,

Until no sign of them, or any sign of any tree, will ever show.

LXVII

Right when you're almost there, on the *top*—you'll fall,

And in the *Hands of Providence* you'll rest your *hopes* and *goals*

And when you're just about of giving up, an *Unseen Hand*

Shall pull your deadweight, back to where you stand.

LXVIII

"To the *Young and Beautiful* I propose a toast!

Now, this very moment, while the time's not lost;

Drink the *cup of pleasures* and the *cup of joys*

For the *Anguish Urn* the *Old Age* employs."

LXIX

The *Climate of the World* will go awry,
The *Evil Sword* shall rule by *evil eye*;
And you—You *fools* who sold the *Planet's Fate*,
Shall beg *Salvation* from the *Seventh Gate*.

LXX

Jealousy! The ever-growing lack of trust

Shall engulf your mind and turn your thoughts to dust;

Burn the fear of losing your loved one and end

That pretended torment that you don't understand.

LXXI

"Into which beauty parlor the oak has trimmed its crown?

Who was the makeup artist who died that green and brown?"

After *one thousand years* its colors never fade,

While painter after painter still *signs* under its shade.

LXXII

"How is it that you see and understand

What Life is all about while we pretend?"

The nightingale cried in jolly flight:

"How is it that we' learned and that you can't?"

QUATRAINS—ECHOES OF EXISTENCE

QUATRAIN LXXI p. 81
[First Color Illustrated Edition]

"Into which beauty parlor the oak has trimmed its crown?
Who was the makeup artist who died that green and brown?"
After *one thousand years* its colors never fade,
While painter after painter still *signs* under its shade.

QUATRAINS—ECHOES OF EXISTENCE

QUATRAIN LXXII p. 121
[First Color Illustrated Edition]

"How is it that you see and understand
What Life is all about while we pretend?"
The nightingale cried in jolly flight:
"How is it that we' learned and that you can't?"

LXXIII

The ruthless force that you may call *'Revenge'*

Shall hatch erratic thoughts and into plots arrange

Perhaps for *'dearest friends'* to *Ruin* and to *Chase*

And *Tear* each other, in a last *embrace*.

LXXIV

If all the people the same *Book* would share

Creativeness would be a climb from *Where?*

The starry candle-lights unnoticed in the sun

Could only stand out if the *Night* is there...

LXXV

Oh! How beguiled *Patience* could get your *Vigor* shuttered

Into the finest ashes and thor'ly be scattered

Over the *Hills of Hopes* and *Will* and *Love*

Until your *Faith* decides, should you be spared or watered.

LXXVI

The nearly withered *Rose* when in the house was brought,

After it had its comfort and gained some strength, it thought

Its precious beauty to protect—in thorns be dressed,

And stung the hand that once nursed and caressed.

LXXVII

And when you'll hear me knocking at your door

Asking '*Forgiveness*' and with love *Implore*

Into the *Temple of Your Heart* to enter—*Please, let me in!*

And I shall leave it empty—*nevermore*.

LXXVIII

Mo matter how flinty you might drive
Your *Luck* out of its corner and survive;
For *Clemency* encore will set you up
And throw your *Fate* against an *Ailing Ride*.

LXXIX

The *woman's sculpture* made of pallid clay
Was finished by the artist the same day;
"Whose *nude* is that?' I asked him. And she moaned:
"I'm Venus! And don't touch me!... Get away!"

LXXX

The *Game of Love* shall last when played in *two*,

If shared fillings match, or if the cards are new;

When played by more, the *King of Hearts* with *Diamonds hand*

Shall win your matching Queen and—*That's the End!*

LXXXI

Neither surprised he was. Nor would he care

To raise his brows and into *Future* stare,

But said, "*I'll see you soon*" and then *asleep he went*;

Not saying *When* we'll meet, and neither *How*, nor *Where*.

LXXXII

Myriad footprints on the sand I saw,

But none to recognize of anyone's I'd know;

Some, rise up their names along their castle's side;

Consumed so rapid by the *waves*, departing with the *tide*.

QUATRAINS—ECHOES OF EXISTENCE

QUATRAIN LXXVII p. 89
[First Color Illustrated Edition]

And when you'll hear me knocking at your door
Asking 'Forgiveness' and with *love* Implore
Into the Temple of Your Heart to enter—Please, let me in!
And I shall leave it empty—nevermore.

QUATRAINS—ECHOES OF EXISTENCE

QUATRAIN LXXXII p. 94
[First Color Illustrated Edition]

Myriad footprints on the sand I saw,
But none to recognize of anyone's I'd know;
Some, rise up their names along their castle's side;
Consumed so rapid by the waves, departing with the tide.

LXXXIII

See there, the *Ashes* of a fire that passed?

Were swept with the first breeze and vanished in the gust;

But when you burn inside, they *stain within*,

And may a lifetime flare, 'til you turn to dust.

LXXXIV

Nothing changed you see, and *Nothing's Learned*:

Wars after wars its generations burned,

And *Peace* was promised as we fight for *Peace*,

While *History* repeats as often as its pages turn.

LXXXV

The *Law* was *verbal-written* for the *Age* to rule
Every single moment you embrace to see;
Even the worshiped *Gods* worn out in memory
Have left to wonder... looking back at *you* and *me*.

LXXXVI

"*Awe*! She's so *young* and *pure* and *divine*
With marble figure dressed in velvet dress;
Her body standing ready to caress...
"*Oh! Wintry trembling hands, which cannot sign...*"

LXXXVII

When *nothing* here by *nothing* there, *scattered*,
It formed a *World of Nothing* among matter;
And shows you how so least existent were
The growing *Kingdoms*, which *they grew forgotten*.

LXXXVIII

The *Clock* is ticking every second: *Snip!*
For every moment passed, one more to *whip*;
The *Time Inventor* never had defined
When not awake—*Where* do these seconds *Sleep?*

LXXXIX

The *Wind of Fate* is blowing strong, my Dear,

So, dress a warmly coat and keep it near

And it will catch you not so bare and plain

When *winter* comes to freeze your *Hopes* and *Tears*.

XC

Wonder how some *fight* and some *ignore*

Into the *Present* and *Future's* core,

Depositing their counts within the *Bank of Time*,

Withdrawing once and speechlessly... withdraw.

XCI

Wild geese upon the water

Wake the hunters in the gutter

With their joyous free display.

Lives exposed are easy prey!

XCII

Each *Reward* comes *after*, not before the bloom.
Look at the apple tree against the April noon;
It's white dazzling flowers inspire the end of May
When petals after petals for its *Glorious Fruit* make room.

QUATRAINS—ECHOES OF EXISTENCE

QUATRAIN XCVI p. 134
[First Color Illustrated Edition]

When you will lose your mind, and hurt someone,
Beware of Yourself, after the fault is done;
The Voice of Conscience somewhere deep and somehow there,
Shall ask, "Where do you go my friend, from here on?"

QUATRAINS—ECHOES OF EXISTENCE

QUATRAIN XCVII p. 113
[First Color Illustrated Edition]

The *Strength of Wonder* on a rustling, ageless sea
Could ignore about the surface the wisest *you* and *me*;
While the cooping hand of *Universe* upholds our Planet's star
Among other zillion Stars—important too, you see...

XCIII

Shaky Hands and *Watery Eyes*
Through old letters wonder-byes;
Seek the memories of the past
Where the teen years *ever lasts*...

XCIV

And soon your *paradise* may seem to come

When so incited you and me shall *pare into one*;

Nearby the scent of lilies, soft melody, and wine'

Awe! Pinch yourself! Should you feel pain, you are
Alive, not *gone*...

XCV

Do not *repel* when hollow fate is deepening,

Nor *weep* upon the stains of your so *destined path*,

Much blazing seems your *Life* after its *Strains* and *Wrath*;

The *Dread of Thunder* once departed *forever* shall be *sleeping*.

XCVI

When you will lose your mind, and hurt someone,
  Beware of Yourself, after the fault is done;
The *Voice of Conscience* somewhere deep and somehow there,
Shall ask, *"Where do you go my friend, from here on?"*

XCVII

The *Strength of Wonder* on a rustling, ageless sea
Could ignore about the surface the wisest *you* and *me*;
While the cooping hand of *Universe* upholds our Planet's star
Among other zillion Stars—important too, you see...

XCVIII

The *Present*, sometimes slow and somehow fast
    Slips into the *Future* and the *Past*,
    The *'very moment' lives* within your reach
As long as filled with *Life* and *made to last*.

XCIX

You know a *Season* when it comes since it warns before it shows,

And once arriving, stays awhile until another comes and goes.

And so, your everyday emotions announce the weather of your moods.

Don't frown and sigh, they're only *Seasons*,

and *Life* with it, it moves... *It moves...*

C

Said someone: "I'd like to climb the stairs
And be the *Pinnacle of Stars* somehow, up there."
A voice cried within, "*Even the stars may Fall!*"
But *where* they'll end up is the question—*Where?*

CI

And *You, Yourselves,* and *Millions of Your Kind,*
With your profound, or lost, or apathetic mind',
Shall give in one by one after your time is done,
To fill the skies with moods of blue *admired by the blind.*

CII

The *Beauty*, the *Softness* and the *Stainless Grace*

Are mere *common weapons* for women to enlace,

They explode within, or outright, from the depths

Of their inner focus, to doom upon your pace.

QUATRAINS—ECHOES OF EXISTENCE

QUATRAIN CXIII p. 133
[First Color Illustrated Edition]

The water trickled from the fountain's crest
Along with thousand years which passed to rest
*"How many lovers by its side set voiceless hopes
Of memories and kissing lips forever pressed?"*

QUATRAINS—ECHOES OF EXISTENCE

QUATRAIN CXXII p. 142
[First Color Illustrated Edition]

I see the World in *Flames*, and *Smoke*, and *Shambles*,
And *Hate among the Kind* where freedom trembles;
I see *Creation* burned and *Shame*, I see
While me and you *re-born* to you and me...

CIII

"How is it that always the vaulting *Nights* and *Days*

Dispute their everlasting divisional displays?"

Erupted one, "*Can't you tell*

That twenty-four hours make a Full Day Spell?"

CIV

Through this *botanic garden* where flowers drift therein

Thousand steps did echo of generations—*in*;

Walking on the shale, whispering vows throughout,

Penned in an image fading of generations—*out*.

CV

Captive Angels suffering and scattered,
Wingless souls so tender 'n' yet so mattered;
Illustrious Names ordered into Flesh
From Dust and Breathe, *"Look how to ashes shuttered!"*

CVI

"The winter blows to freeze December rains"
Hinted the twigs tapping against my panes;
And then the *Spirit of the Winter* called:
"Let's see who stays this time... Let's see who goes..."

CVII

At the same *country Lodge* where numerous checked in,

On the same berth and mattress that comforted Mark Twain,

Also slept you so lost and spent, but *"How many of you have heard*

The voices of Tom Sawyer calling and Huckleberry Finn?"

CVIII

"Oh, *Love*! How is it that you pretend to heal

The deepest wounds instilled in us? And figure then to steal

Our only *hope*, eternally branded into our *souls* and *senses*:

Immortal faith and *dazzled smiles* broken on *false pretenses*?"

CIX

Compare not the very moment, for the next one could easily bring

For Some *King* to be a *Beggar* and some *Beggar* be a *King*'

Look upon yourself and wonder if you awe yourself or not.

Life is Hope, a *String of Wonders* that you must work at *knot by knot*.

CX

How many sweethearts have you embraced with winning love and care

That you would like now to recall just for a moment's spare?

To *Hold* and *Taste* and *Feel* their heat and *Melt* within their souls...

You shot your eyes and call their names,

But where they are—Who knows?

CXI

The seasoned humpback *beggar* lowly dressed in putrid duds

Espied from the distant corner about the tavern's feasting crowds;

I quickly gave some cash to him and food to him I brought;

The moving crowds have vanished, but *his semblance ever not.*

CXII

Some *proof* of *Universal Love* you had reached and reaped

Into our heart part emptiness eagerly poured it down and dipped;

Grew there a vibrant splendor of a lovey-dovey crop

Whose indoors are swept by cherished, piece by piece, and drop by drop.

QUATRAINS—ECHOES OF EXISTENCE

QUATRAIN CXXX p. 152
[First Color Illustrated Edition]

The *Greatest Show on Earth* might have begun
As *Cash* and *Putrid* share *the World* as *One*,
The *Opera of Mankind* will erupt to see
At *Genesis* Horizon—*Apocalypse* for *Dawn*.

QUATRAINS—ECHOES OF EXISTENCE

QUATRAIN CXXXIX p. 164
[First Color Illustrated Edition]

I heard your whispers while I was asleep
The *Ocean* told you that she heard my *weep*.
It wasn't *I* lamenting—but your *Cup*
Who thought I drank your wine and drowned in its deep.

CXIII

The water trickled from the fountain's crest

Along with thousand years which passed to rest;

"How many lovers by its side set voiceless hopes

Of memories and kissing lips forever pressed?"

CXVI

Love–A solid bridge between two roads

Whose *two-way path* is crossed by many loads,

Abolished not by any *Force* we know;

Eternally carved into our hearts avow.

CXV

You and *Yourself*, the both of you—*Be strong!*

Awake from weakness. Turn what's *Right* from *Wrong.*

The '*Friends*' you thought you had now let you down,

So, *tear up this page and write a better song!*

CXVI

Of what it was a little but remained,

The most of thy experience 'twas ordained.

"Whatever written it will come to pass," quoth he

A thousand years ago. And his words never waned.

CXVII

Among the crowds I roam and lost I get,

And raft among the shades not rotted yet

Of knowing not where going, hence afar

I think my *alter ego* had been let.

CXVIII

Youth—Just a *teasing pattern* shaped by our life's display

With everlasting feelings of an *Eternal Force*

Impressed throughout the *Veil of Time*, then to divorce

For never to re-marry, until you're *Old* and *Grey*...

CXIX

Look for the *Reason on all Things*, my Love,

And seek the *Truth* around you and *Above*.

The *earthly pleasures* of this life embrace,

For once departed, you may leave no trace...

CXX

Of *instant money*, many a word 'been told

Since the beholder never could behold;

For *cursed the pelf* obtained by *easy gains*,

To which so many their souls have sold.

CXXI

Between the *Day* and *Night*—a foggy line,

Running along the *Dusk* and the *Divine*

Upon where WE ALL walk *one way* until exhausted,

To fall then to a side *to which inclined*...

CXXII

I see the World in *Flames*, and *Smoke*, and *Shambles*,
And *Hate among the Kind* where freedom trembles;
I see *Creation* burned, and *Shame* I see
While me and you *re-born* to you and me...

QUATRAINS—ECHOES OF EXISTENCE

QUATRAIN CXLIII p. 170
[First Color Illustrated Edition]

All lifetime dreams—a phantom-like display.
All promises of mankind—the breath of yesterday.
All matter and non-matter—the essence of your thoughts
All hopes and aspirations—a moment of delay.

QUATRAINS—ECHOES OF EXISTENCE

QUATRAIN CXLVIII p. 124
[First Color Illustrated Edition]

And then she poured *wine* into my vintage *Urn*
And played *soft music*; and by my side did *burn*
  Of *Ecstasy*, and *Love*, and *wholesome Youth*,
As if she knew those *moments*—never shall return.

CXXIII

Along the *Path of Truth* a flickering flame:

Uncertainty. *"Behold!"* said one, "The *Blame*

"Falls on some *Eve and her beloved Adam! Right?"*

"Revile no one my friend. We're all the same..."

CXXIV

Said the Saint: *"Believe, and you'll not Fall!"*

Behind, another voice swearing, *"We all*

Must take a Chance: Sell or Be Sold..."

And then—the *Values* of our *Conscience* called...

CXXV

Life—The smallest part of our existence' site.
Death—The path for us to reach the *Earnest Light*;
Shapes without detail, brightness without hue,
Restated by the *Master* who molds it into view.

CXXVI

The World—A molded ball on which like dust
We are all scattered layers upon crust.
Above—the Hand of the Magician drew, and *signed*,
Then kicked it back into the *Universal Lost*.

CXXVII

With my own *Hope*, I spoke today in a disputing kind

About the *Heavens* somewhere there, and of the *Loam* behind;

My *hope* replied, *"Look up and seek and Tell how far you see"*

But there stood '*Night* staring at me, as if to pity me.

CXXVIII

My mother's teardrop—an infinite of pain;
The never-ending story of sunshine and of rain,
On which a thousand vessels had sailed filled with dreams
And yet another thousand were never seen again...

CXXIX

Within ourselves—a world extreme; a Firmament so blind;

Outside—another infinite to hold our very kind;

The Elixir of Life you seek is in the *Well of Thought,*

Yet, oomph dissolves not by the law, but from the set of mind.

CXXX

The *Greatest show on Earth* might have began
As *Cash* and *Putrid* shares *the World* as *One*,
The *Opera of Mankind* will erupt to see
At *Genesis* horizon—*Apocalypse* for *Dawn*.

CXXXI

Oh, Mother! . . . Father . . . Here I come,

I've done much of *Nothing* and lots of it I've done;

Besides me 'let my spirit to guard over my kin

For then to rest forever within their souls *as One*.

CXXXII

Ephemeral creatures, are we not?

Epitome of *Trials* that Providence forgot;

And shadows from traces of "*Present and the Past*"

Treat our births with *cheers*, with *ashes*, and with Dust.

QUATRAINS—ECHOES OF EXISTENCE

QUATRAIN CLVI p. 185
[First Color Illustrated Edition]

Your *body* next to mine in an *Eternal Hold*,
A glass of wine of red grape to uphold;
From *dusk* till *dawn*, our *Hearts* and *Selves* will blend
To write the best love story *Ever Told*.

QUATRAINS—ECHOES OF EXISTENCE

QUATRAIN CLIX p. 197
[First Color Illustrated Edition]

The stars are *winking* from the skies tonight
   Reflecting in your eyes a brighter light;
Let's kiss in this euphoric moment *mon amour*,
Before the *Dawn of Day* shall end our *endless night*.

CXXXII

Ephemeral creatures, are we not?

Epitome of *Trials* that Providence forgot;

And shadows from traces of "*Present and the Past*"

Treat our births with *cheers*, with *ashes*, and with Dust.

CXXXIII

Today, I lost my friend to *Faith* dispute, you see;

He—a *Believer* and I—a *Thought Recruit* to be;

He said— "*The Maker* has the *Key* to all your *Doubts*"

I asked in awe— "He gave it to you and denied it me?"

CXXXIV

You cannot stop a stormy wind to blow

No matter *Who* you are or *What* you know;

And you can't swerve its course—despite your *Will*;

Nor thousand wills could make its *Story* go....

CXXXV

Do what you *Love* to do in *Life*, my dear;

Follow your dreams whether they're *far* or *near*;

Those *Doubts* that cloud your mind are only there

To *try* your *Courage* against the ending *Fears*.

CXXXVI

"I do not know *You*, my dear *God—My Lord*"

"The *God of Conscience* crippled by a Word"

"You shalt not *Kill*" and yet—*Annihilation*

Is written in *Your Blood* and rendered through *Your Sword*.

CXXXVII

Isn't it strange how *Yesterdays* are forever gone?

It feels as if an *Instant* paused, and then that instant ran

Without a trace, taking along... *Centuries of Yore*.

We're quarreling like sages yet *perish—one by one*.

CXXXVIII

Oh! Come to me and share my cup of *Love*

While there's still *Youth*, rush to my behove;

The time is trickling through the *Sandglass* lip

As our lips fade kisses, sweet-ended, thereof.

CXXXIX

I heard your whispers while I was asleep

The *Ocean* told you that she heard my *weep*.

It wasn't *I* lamenting—but your *Cup*

Who thought I drank your wine and drowned in its deep.

CXL

To the *Religious* and the *Atheist*—Lo!

Your candles render but a *Shadow-Show*

Of your obscure *Life*—until your *Flames* are gone;

Chanced by the *Time Inventor*, far beyond and long ago.

CXLI

Well, said another while I was *Depressed*:

Waste not a second of your time invest

In grief, for you are but a *Cloud*

Whose shadow leaves no trace on *Earthly Breast*.

QUATRAINS—ECHOES OF EXISTENCE

QUATRAIN CLXXXIV p. 219
[First Color Illustrated Edition]

When the Old Age, the *Course of Time*, sneaks in,
With wrinkles, watery eyes, and pains within,
My *Hourglass of Time* shaped like a woman
Will make me think of you an endless dream.

QUATRAINS—ECHOES OF EXISTENCE

QUATRAIN CLXXXIV p. 206
[First Color Illustrated Edition]

I shall traverse the *Vastness* of the *Sky*
And leave behind a *World of Dust* and *Clay*
I'll see *Time* stretching, shrinking, breathing *LIFE*
While I'll be none but *Love* and *Thought*, one *Day*...

CXLII

He ventured loudly— "*None* of what you see is True"

"*Life*'s not endless, and *Death* is but a moment, too."

"They score a millisecond in the *Eternal mix*"

"Of *Motions* and *Illusions*, which are *ALL* part of *You*.

CXLIII

All lifetime dreams—a phantom-like display.

All promises of mankind—the breath of yesterday.

All matter and nonmatter—the essence of your thoughts'

All hopes and aspirations—a moment of delay.

CXLIV

And when a thousand years from today shall pass

Into the infinite *Creation's* incongruous morass

The World as seen today with its convulsing *Ego*

Shall be no more, alike the *wine* in your *abandoned glass*.

CXLV

And when the *Chains of Fate* will break your moral veins

You'll be denied, and lonely, among your *trials* and *pains*.

Behind your mental bars you'll wither like a *Rose*

Whose stabbing spines are all that's left from its long gone remains.

CXLVI

"*Religion!*" One roared. "*The attribute of Pride!*"

"The only *Seal of Honor* from which you must not hide"

"Should be the very *Clearance* to sate your *Moral Stains.*"

"*Then, have pity on nonconformists,*" my Conscience replied.

CXLVII

"Where have you been, my friend. You're *grey* and *thin*,"

"You've *aged* since last I've seen you. How have you been?"

Said I – "We drank together a pot of wine *last night;*"

"You were no more than *Twenty*, and I was *Seventeen*...."

CXLVIII

And then she poured *wine* into my vintage *Urn*

And played *soft music*; and by my side did *burn*

Of *Ecstasy*, and *Love*, and *wholesome Youth*,

As if she knew those *moments*—never shall return.

CXLIX

The *Secret of Eternal Life* she found

Las night, when raptured in embraces she was bound.

"Is she a *Mortal,* or *Goddess Incarnate?*"

"Or was our wine—too *lilting* and *profound?*"

CL

The *Voice* in my Dream, wailed "*It's too Late*"

"*To overturn and to recast the Human Fate!*"

The *Masters of the Earth—Degenerate Few*

Learnt ~ either *Rule*, or else ... *Obliterate*.

CLI

For what is *Love* if not a *Cup of Joy*

A *Garland of Surprises* among *Life's* pleasing *Toys*

You see, One Day, I woke up in the night

To realize that all t'was but a ploy.

QUATRAINS—ECHOES OF EXISTENCE

QUATRAIN CLXXXIV p. 182
[First Color Illustrated Edition]

The *Moon and Stars*, their silent watch do keep
While weary mortals close their eyes in sleep
But some awake to gaze upon the sky
And wonder at the secrets that make *Heavens* weep...

QUATRAINS—ECHOES OF EXISTENCE

QUATRAIN LXXXIV p. 98
[First Color Illustrated Edition]

Nothing changed, you see, and *Nothing's Learned*:
Wars after wars its generations burned,
And *Peace* was promised as we fight for *Peace*,
While *History* repeats as often as its pages turn.

CLII

A *Ruby* – A True Friendship in this World

It glows with *Good* amid the *Evil's Thrall*

Yet, *Fate* may hurl its bolts and shake its *Pearl*

As *Falsehood* may unloose its golden *Ball*.

CLIII

The *Moon and Stars* their silent watch do keep

While weary mortals close their eyes in sleep

But some awake to gaze upon the sky

And wonder at the secrets that make *Heavens* weep...

CLIV

The *Rose of Youth* blooms only for a Day

And soon its petals *wither* and *decay*.

We cannot keep its *fragrance* or its *hue*,

But only sigh and watch it fade away.

CLV

Time flies – like an arrow in the sky,

We watch it pass and wonder *where* it *flies*;

Waste not a second but rush and grab the *Gift*

To *Live*, and *Love*, and *Laugh*, then say *Goodbye*.

CLVI

Your *body* next to mine in an *Eternal Hold*,

A glass of wine of red grape to uphold;

From *dusk* till *dawn*, our *Hearts* and *Selves* will blend

To write the best love story *Ever Told*.

CLVII

And so, you lashed your fellow man with bane,

And left him in a *trail of blood* and *pain*,

— Have you just, for a moment, contemplate

The *Price* you'll pay for all your *Selfish Gain?*

CLVIII

Last night, I dreamt I bid *farewell* my lover

It left me empty and alone, yet sober;

The *Wine of Life* no more shall fill the cup

That got us drunk with *Passions* to discover.

CLIX

The stars are *winking* from the skies tonight

Reflecting in your eyes a brighter light;

Let's kiss in this euphoric moment *mon amour*,

Before the *Dawn of Day* shall end our *endless night*.

CLX

The *Road to Victory* may be *Long* and *Hard*

As you may run against the *hurdles' guard*

Yet, once *determined* to attain your Goal

Don't stop until you win your *Final Card*.

CLXI

You may have *failed* a *Thousand Fails* before

Wanting to *give it up*: shotting the door;

Awe! Let not have your Fears define your *Fate*

For once a Winner, you'll be poor—*no more*.

QUATRAINS—ECHOES OF EXISTENCE

QUATRAIN LXXXIV p. 102
[First Color Illustrated Edition]

The *Clock* is ticking every second: *Snip!*
For every moment passed, one more to *whip*;
The *Time Inventor* never had defined
When not awake—*Where* do these seconds *Sleep?*

QUATRAINS—ECHOES OF EXISTENCE

QUATRAIN LXXXIV p. 86
[First Color Illustrated Edition]

If all the people the same *Book* would share
Creativeness would be a climb from *Where?*
The starry candle-lights unnoticed in the sun
Could only stand out if the *Night* is there...

CLXII

LIFE is *too short* to waste on *vain pursuits*

Or chase the shadows of the *Worldly Fruits*

Behold! The Happiness that only lasts,

Lives in your *Soul* and in your *Love's Salutes*.

CLXIII

The *Book of Fate* is written by the *Pen*

But none can read its *hidden meaning* when

We open it with Fear or Doubt or Hope

Only to find a *riddle* now and then.

CLXIV

The *Friend in Need* is oft' a *traitor's seed*

Who wounds you with a *dagger* or a *reed*;

You know not of his *Malice* or his *Guile*

But you will feel the *smearing of the bleed*.

CLXV

The Spring has come and filled the air with scent

The *nightingale* sings of love and lament

Come, *fill the cup*, and drink the *Wine of Life*

For who knows when the hour of death is sent?

CLXVI

The stars are shining in the vault of *Heaven*

The moon is smiling on the earth below;

Do tell me, where are those to you who seek the truth

Yet, lie beyond the realm of *sight* and *show*?

CLXVII

And so the *Rose* that's blooming in its fair

Inspires the *nightingale* concerting his mate;

Lo! How the *Rose* will fade and disappear

And how his *Soul*, like mine, shall mourn his *Fate*.

CLXVIII

Oh, dear friend! Depression can be Scary

But do not let it make you feel so weary

For there is Hope and Joy beyond the Gloom;

Follow your dreams and find your lucky Fairy.

CLXIX

Life—but a *journey* full of *twists* and *turns*;

From whom, we learn our steps of *falls* and *burns*;

Yet, sometimes, we forget our *moral sense*

While ' *Gods are weeping* when history returns.

CLXX

So, you may think *Revenge* shall make it *Right*

When, in the end, it only breeds more *Spite?*

Oh, poor You — how desperate is your claim

As to not know the *Daylight* from the *Night*.

CLXXI

Last night I dreamt I bid farewell my lover

It left me empty, and alone, yet sober;

The Wine of Life no more shall fill the cup

That got us drunk with passions to *discover*...

QUATRAINS—ECHOES OF EXISTENCE

QUATRAIN CLX p. 201
[First Color Illustrated Edition]

So, you may think *Revenge* shall make it *Right*
When, in the end, it only breeds more *Spite*?
Oh, *poor You* — how desperate is your claim
As to not know the *Daylight* from the *Night*.

QUATRAINS—ECHOES OF EXISTENCE

QUATRAIN CLX p. 207
[First Color Illustrated Edition]

In this *Great Expanse* of endless Stars and Gleam
The Universe itself: an endless *Stretching Dream*
Of *timeless boundaries*. And yet, my friend— Behold!
There's something even larger—*Stupidity Extreme*...

CLXXII

Within the *Tapestry of Time*, your final place,

Amidst the stars, in cosmic endless space,

You'll leave behind the *joys* and *pains* you've known,

And find your *Solace* in Its *Last Embrace*.

CLXXIII

I shall traverse the *Vastness* of the *Sky*

And leave behind a *World of Dust* and *Clay*

I'll see *Time* stretching, shrinking, breathing LIFE

While I'll be none but *Love* and *Thought*, one *Day*...

CLXXIV

In this *Great Expanse* of endless Stars and Gleam

The Universe itself: an endless *Stretching Dream*

Of *timeless boundaries*. And yet, my friend— Behold!

There's something even larger—*Stupidity Extreme...*

CLXXV

For such is *LIFE*—a *canvas* sprinkled with Hopes and Treasures

Alike a Turkish carpet — a *Caravan of Pleasures*

Where you and I get oft'n lost, yet find ourselves again

In Eve's and Adam's clothes —poor *Angels* without feathers.

CLXXVI

Upon this *endless stage* where Fate and Daydreams chase

In this Life's fleeting twirls as round and round we pace

Let this be our anthem to share with the youth:

"Be ashamed to die without a *Win* for *Human Race*".

CLXXVII

In *Castle's* halls where whispers come and go

Fear not the *Darkness*, for it's a *Magic Show*

Whereby the *Count of Malefaction* 'll dare your Strength,

As you'll decide who'll win, and whom you'll want to go.

CLXXVIII

The Good you do may breed Envy, anon.

And turn your Blessing to a biting Scorn.

You look not for a Meed or Recompense.

Yet, brace yourself with none but Wrath or Scorn.

CLXXIX

So, in the midst of gloom, do not despair,

But let your dreams take flight; ignore dark's stare,

Embrace the light that guides your Instinct's path

And with your Faerie's wings, fear not to dare.

CLXXX

The Vine of Love is sweeter than the Grape:

The *Grape of Passion* pulped into Wine and Shape.

—O, how I care not for tomorrow's vows

When now, we're locked in Love without escape...

CLXXXI

Did you see the Bird of Life again this Spring?

It swiftly carries *spells* on every wing.

We see not whence it comes nor where it goes.

But only hear the fleeting cries it sings.

QUATRAINS—ECHOES OF EXISTENCE

QUATRAIN CLXXXIII p. 218
[First Color Illustrated Edition]

For what is Happiness, given that Life is Short,
If not a *fleeting moment* of some sort?
A moment where the Universe resides
And *all there is to be* is none but HOPE...

QUATRAINS—ECHOES OF EXISTENCE

QUATRAIN CXXXIV p. 160
[First Color Illustrated Edition]

Do what you *Love* to do in *Life*, my dear;
Follow your dreams, whether they're *far* or *near*;
Those *Doubts* that cloud your mind are only there
To try your *Courage* against the ending *Fears*.

CLXXXII

The World may seem a Dark and Dreary place.

But do not let *Despair* your Spirit chase.

For in your heart, there burns a *Fiery Flame*

Where you'll find Hope and Passion, and ... *your Grace*.

CLXXXIII

For what is Happiness, given that Life is Short,

If not a *fleeting moment* of some sort?

A moment where the Universe resides.

And *all there is to be* is none but HOPE...

CLXXXIV

When the Old Age, the *Course of Time*, sneaks in,

With wrinkles, watery eyes, and pains within,

My *Hourglass of Time* shaped like a woman

Will make me think of you an endless dream.

CLXXXV

She said, "I love your Verses, and I like your Wine.

I find in them the *Touch of the Divine.*"

My Love! Neither the verses nor the wine you taste

Are mine, but *our Reflections in the Breath of Time!*

CLXXXVI

I see the Morning blushing, watching our Youth in *spree*,

Upon Dawn's flying moments, which make Eternity,

While with the purest feelings, our Hearts compose and bleed

Music made of happy tears. Oh, what a lovely Symphony...

CLXXXVII

A Statue of cold *Image* and yet, charmingly warm,

As if the Gods have made her in their Shape and Form.

Perhaps now incarnated to tempt the world in sin,

And then back to the *carving* forever she'll return.

CLXXXVIII

'Tis but a fleeting life, you see—a Fate sublime

As for Humanity, we chase a *fervid dream*:

To leave a *Victory* for those who want to learn

That without *Light*, a *shadow* cannot win.

CLXXXIX

Hey, you! who look like humans but are not humane,

Yes, you, the *Parasites of ' Human Race to Blame*:

For all the Wars and Suffering, Famine and Death,

May you be cursed by ' Gods to LIVE and DIE in *Shame*!

QUATRAINS—ECHOES OF EXISTENCE

QUATRAIN CLXXXIX p. 224
[First Color Illustrated Edition]

Hey, you! who look like humans but are not humane,
 Yes, you, the *Parasites of ' Human Race to Blame*:
For all the Wars and Suffering, Famine and Death,
May you be cursed by ' Gods to LIVE and DIE in *Shame*!

QUATRAINS—ECHOES OF EXISTENCE

About the Author

C.S. Douglas is a multifaceted American writer, poet, and entrepreneur. Recognized for his unique cross-genre style and nonfiction novels, Douglas has showcased his versatility as a novelist, poet, screenwriter, playwright, lyricist, and composer. A deep influence from the poetic verses of Omar Khayyam resonates in his writings, yet Douglas stands out by often breaking traditional rubaiyat metrics, infusing originality into every piece.

With a life dedicated to the literary arts and fostering global author communities, C.S. Douglas remains a beacon of innovation and profound creativity in contemporary literature.

QUATRAINS—ECHOES OF EXISTENCE

Editorial Reviews

C.S. Douglas writes quatrains in a time where endless, vapid, self-aggrandizing mediated words and images have been normalized for profit. Disinformation lurks around every print and digital corner. Some platforms expand their bandwidth (scroll after scroll after scroll), while others limit output to a set number of characters (-5 words over the limit, in red). The veracity and tenacity of an argument may be created, mediated, distributed, and hidden by artificial intelligence. The oldest philosophical, poetic, literary, and political questions (e.g., "What is real?" and "How do I live?") dominate all media. And yet the answers to such near-eternal questions tend to bleed cliché or celebrate generalization in deeply unsatisfying and spiritually toxic ways.

Humanity is in trouble. What is to be done? How do we communicate our truths, our worldviews, our impressions and suspicions, and deepest truths inside this cabal of communicative plague? *Quatrains: Echoes of Existence* offers one of the oldest, clearest, and most elaborate answers (and analgesics) by way of aphorism, one of the oldest Western poetic intelligence and source code for creative inspiration and expression with deep ties to the Japanese haiku. Both quatrain and haiku emerged during times of great political and cultural upheaval. The same can be said for C.S. Douglas' bold yet humble project.

Beginning with lamentation and ending with spiritual restitution, the first ten quatrains balance majesty and humility, each line serving as *vox clemantis in deserto* (a voice crying out in the wilderness). Life and death play games as we mere mortals grow more concerned about the quality and quiddity of our lives every minute of every day, and yet C.S. Douglas demands that we take careful enjoyment in "The life that's given" (III). A Biblical riff announces the depth of Douglas' meditative aphorism as a warning against the temptation to know (to obsess over) life and death and strive for (to obsess over), above all things, the knowledge of Good and Evil. The defiant approach to the world's mysteries, terrors, and joys did not bode well for the first humans, even though breaking prelapsarian chains was absolutely necessary to free humanity from eternal subservience. "Now what?" Douglas seems to ask.

Slowly, the verses transition from lyric and epic to a deeply personal emphasis on existential matters clashing with eternity: "Why bother measuring the time? / There's No Beginning and No End (VI). The Creator, the Omniscient Voice, perhaps even a simple Prime Mover responds with a loving embrace and attempts to assure the receiver of these cosmic and everyday intelligent and creative challenges to pay close attention: as hints, echoes, windfall secrets are whispered, "I love you to a never-ending!" (VII). "Live these words," Douglas insists. Contemplate both their meaning and their ineffable cadence in a manner "[w]here memories come back and stay / And 'thousand years a minute seems" (VIII).

It is vital that the reader, the audience (mere mortals we) ingest and integrate and digest everyday experiences and emotions ("To Love, and Kiss, and Play and Pull and Reap," VIII) so we can balance our doubts and fears with courage and clarity, with an acceptance of the meager approximations and half-hearted attempts to understand our existence. Douglas challenges us to remember and celebrate how "Life is winding / As we seem so far away / And yet so close to the final answer / Which divides the night and day" (X).

With such philosophical and poetic depth and such a unique challenge to humanity in its moment of mediated paralysis and endless, painful noise, it is easy to imagine how (in an alternative timeline, another universe) this project would have easily drawn the attention of editors at the Loeb Classics; they would have mistaken C.S. Douglas' poetry for a long-lost manuscript authored by Horace or Seneca. This book is not only an unexpected gift to the world but an invitation for all to better understand how ancient modes of thinking and creating can inoculate us from the kind of anxiety and despair centuries of the modern project expect us to treat as a baseline and not as an aberration.

—Robert Craig Baum

I was fascinated by hearing the first few verses of this epic challenge. I was completely hooked on the style and temperament when I heard the second set. One minute, you feel you understand sentiments from a time gone by, and then in the next line, you are smacked into the present. I feel we will see a bestseller cult status in the not-too-distant future. C.S. Douglas has kept this from us for many years, and it is right to release it now.

This series will relax you, make you feel something from afar that might not be explained, and yet you sense you are in good hands. A worthy contribution to an ever-growing appreciation of poetry and prose in the 21st century.

—Lee Benson

The ineffable words of C.S. Douglas spring from the page like a songbird's tune, enlightening the receiver's ears. Beautifully executed. The verses echo the great classics of a bygone era -

—D.G. Torrens

Are quatrains an extinct literary style? C.S. Douglas, a sensible soul with epic talent, has reached a milestone in his literary career with Quatrains: Echo of Existence. Pain, happiness, deception, and our humanness displayed through chiseled, felt-through words morphed into quatrains. A real enjoyment to read and a thoughtful gift."

—Claudiu Murgan